Happy Birthday

W9-BRH-811

IT!

DRAW

BUILD IT!

I LOVE YOU

BAKE IT!

STENCIL IT!

DO IT!

Mary Engelbreit's
SPRING

Mary Engelbreit's
SPRING
CRAFT BOOK

Illustrated by Mary Engelbreit
Written by Charlotte Lyons
Photography by Barbara Elliott Martin

ANDREWS AND MCMEEL
A Universal Press Syndicate Company
Kansas City

is a registered trademark of
Mary Engelbreit Enterprises, Inc.

10 9 8 7 6 5 4 3 2 1

Library of Congress Cataloging-in-Publication Data

Engelbreit, Mary.
    Mary Engelbreit's spring craft book / illustrated by Mary
  Engelbreit ; written by Charlotte Lyons ; photography by
  Barbara Elliott Martin.
      p. cm.
    ISBN 0-8362-2885-5 (hd)
    1. Handicraft. 2. Spring I. Lyons, Charlotte. II. Title.
  TT157.E52 1997
  745.5-dc20   96-38490
                                                        CIP

Design by Stephanie Raaf

Contents

one.
GARDENING

Sun Hat

*Greet the first blade of spring green
in a lovely hat that can be decorated in less time
than it takes to find your gardening gloves.*

A simple straw hat becomes a garden bonnet
with a few artistic accents. Make a hatband
from a length of ribbon or a strip of cotton yard
goods. A five-inch-wide strip can be hemmed, cut
with pinking shears, or just torn on the weave. Tie it
around the hat and secure it with a bow or a knot. A
pretty silk corsage flower from a vintage shop is
pinned to the knot for an old-fashioned look.

Gardener's Basket

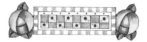

*Organize and ornament a work area
with a decorated basket for seeds and tools.*

A wicker letter basket makes a great catchall
for gardeners' odds and ends. It only takes
a little fancying up with felt flowers and leaves
glued to the front of the basket. Seam-binding
tape combined with rickrack trims the edges.
Fish a ribbon hanger through the back and find
an inviting spot by the door where you can hang
it—or fill it with tools and seed packets as a gift
for a friend.

Watering Can

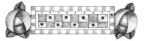

*Paint a watering can
with the spirited colors of spring!*

A plain watering can becomes a gardener's centerpiece with a few strokes of acrylic paint.
Spray paint the can in a base color you like and then
spark it up with painted-on fun. Paint pens are great
for detail; repeat patterns make the most of big
spaces. Don't forget the handle and the spout. Be
sure to seal the finished design with an acrylic sealer to keep your work garden-fresh.

Porch Perches

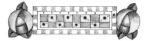

When you spruce up your porch this spring,
cluster your favorite birdhouses
in a cheerful corner.

Any charming collectible would work, but there is something about handmade birdhouses that captures our imaginations and adds a cozy bit of folk art fun. Use old ones from flea markets or new ones made by clever artisans. Look for houses with a common link such as color, material, or shape. Mix and match them on a tabletop or shelf for a village collection.

Home Tweet Home

*Make your own collectible birdhouse
and hang it from a spring arbor.*

There are lots of plain birdhouses at the craft or hardware store that welcome a little special attention to become fairy-tale dwellings. Use acrylic paints and fine tipped brushes to scatter little flowers and dots on the front. Painted shutters, hand-lettering, and a chimney do the rest to make this an endearing garden decoration.

two.
EASTER

Easter Eggs

Cleverness and charm transform these eggs
into astonishing ornaments for the holiday.

L ittle trimmings from the craft store are all one needs for these egg creations. An egg-turned-tiny-teapot has a band of silk rosebuds and pearls. Wheels, a hitch, and a window box dress up an Airstream trailer egg. Another egg wrapped with string becomes a beehive set in a little garden. Paint, charms, hot glue, and a steady hand turn the ordinary into the eggs-traordinary.

Cookie Pot

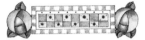

*For an unusual Easter basket, plant
a painted pot with decorated sugar cookies.*

Start by sealing the inside and outside of a
clay pot with acrylic sealer that will keep
the moisture from seeping through. Then paint
the pot with the colors of your choice and a
design such as the one shown here. Fill it with
soil and wheat grass. Wheat grass is available
already grown at a natural foods store. Make
frosted sugar cookies on bamboo skewers and
stick them into the pot as if they might have real-
ly sprouted there.

Holiday Collecting

Bring out a theme collection and create a tabletop arrangement that will delight your family and friends.

Flea market treasures can be mixed in with new Easter collectibles to make an enchanted scene that celebrates the holiday and all its sweetness. Greeting cards, decorated eggs, bunnies, and bonnets nestle together with straw hats and family photographs. A pitcher full of spring's glorious blooms adds vitality and a profusion of vivid color. For anyone who collects, this will be as much fun to create as it is to admire.

Easter Bonnet

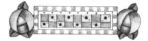

*Make the most of a purchased hat
with a simple appliqué.*

A child's sunbonnet takes on extra charm with a
quick appliquéd rabbit cut from felt or fleece.
Cotton print is stitched onto the brim for a hillside,
and the rabbit is blanket-stitched there, too. A yard
or so of wire-edged ribbon makes a bow and several
little flowers. Make these by wrapping and twisting
the ribbon a few times to build a rosebud effect.
Stitch them in place around the design and add a
few felt leaves around the flowers.

easter

Handkerchief Collar

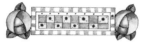

*A vintage handkerchief becomes
an adorable collar for a spring dress.*

Beautiful hankies from long ago are still easy to
find in thrift stores and at flea markets. Perhaps
you have one from your mother or grandmother that
has sentimental value. Choose a child's dress and pin
the hankie onto the collar to see how it will fit. When
you have it positioned correctly from both sides,
mark the opening to be cut away at the neck and at
the back. Before cutting it, use a fine satin or zigzag
stitch to outline the cutting lines. Carefully cut away
the center and opening at the back close to the stitching. Tack the new collar in place.

Bunny Purse

*Surprise someone special
with this child's pocket purse.*

Cut two shapes from acrylic fleece for the body of the purse and two more from another fabric for the lining. Decorate one fleece shape with embroidery and appliqués for the face. Right sides together, sew the lining on the two long sides and across the bottom. Repeat for the fleece. Turn the fleece right side out and insert the unturned lining. Cut two ears and pinch them at the bottom to give them extra body. Pin them to the face between the bag and the lining. Cut a length of ribbon for a handle and stitch in place with the ears. Fold down the raw edges and blindstitch the top of the lining to the top of the bag. Add a big bowtie hand-stitched at the neck.

Cookies and Cakes

Frosted cookies and cupcakes
will be the highlight of the dessert table.

P lain sugar cookies cut in the shapes of bunnies and chicks wear frosted costumes made from tinted icing. Use a pastry tube to make flowers, zigzags, hearts, and bonnets on each. The cupcakes are baked in an egg-shaped pan and frosted with brightly colored icing. Each is rimmed with a grassy green band of frosting.

The heart of the giver makes the gift dear & precious ·LUTHER·

three.
MAY DAY

May Basket

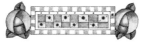

*May Day is a traditional day
of spring celebration.
Bring some of the glistening blooms
into your home with this garden basket.*

hoose a basket to fit on your windowsill, or on a table as a centerpiece, if you prefer. Fit it with a liner and floral oasis that is well soaked in water. Begin with cut flowers (collected in the early morning or evening) that will create height and strength for the rest of the arrangement. If the stems are woody, strip the bark and crush the ends to increase their ability to take in water. Fill in with other flowers wherever needed to fully pack the basket with color. Foliage is an important complement, so be sure to include several branches of green.

Tea Cozy

Make this little cottage to keep your teapot warm while you enjoy tea with a friend.

Use a simple tea cozy pattern, but adapt the style with appliqués and fancy stitching to make it look like a cottage. Before assembling, decorate the plain tea cozy front with a dormer, a country-red door, and curtained windows cut from cotton scraps. Adding a button doorknob and embroidered posies in the window box makes this a dressed-up version of an old favorite.

Spring Wreath

Fashion this quick wreath from a basket of colorful fabric scraps.

Although this wreath was made from vintage handkerchiefs, eight-inch squares of patterned fabrics would do beautifully. Begin by making the fabrics into bunchy flowers. Hold the four corners of the square and make a parachute. Poke the center of the square into your hand and secure the ends with a rubber band. Using a grapevine or willow wreath as the base, stick the fabric bundles right into the wreath all around. Then simply fill in with silk leaf stems around the outside and inside.

for MOTHER O'MINE

four.
MOTHER'S
DAY

Breakfast

Instead of breakfast in bed, set a colorful table where everyone can gather round to sing the praises of good ol' Mom!

Whether Mom goes to work or stays home, everyday dishes set with dish towels as placemats bring a familiar charm to the family table. Bright colors and patterns welcome decorative collectibles like little houses and doll furniture. Cheerfulness and homegrown fun make this a delightful table where everyone can feel comfortable and special at the same time.

44

Mother Dear

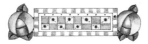

*Make the most of her star status
and collect vintage poems celebrating
the virtues of motherhood.*

Popular as sentimental gifts for Mother then and now, the appeal of these framed poems increases with the years. Keep your eye out for them at flea markets and antique shows. In a dressing room, they combine with a collection of old cosmetic tins for a nostalgic reminder of the joy of mothering.

Sweetheart Pin

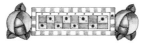

*A baby picture of Dad becomes a treasured
pin for Mom.*

Make a print of an old photograph and find a
little frame at the craft store that fits the
image. Cut a piece of acetate to protect the photograph in the frame. Arrange this on a piece of mat
board or cardboard that you can cover with fabric
or buttons to dress it up. From the bottom, hang a
sweetheart charm and glue a pin back to the back of
the mat board.

Cookbook Slipcover

*A tattered favorite gets a new look
with an easy-to-sew slipcover.*

Wrap the cookbook in a piece of fabric that has been cut larger than the book. Allow 1/2-inch overlap on the top and bottom and 4 inches at the cover edges. Finish the inside edges before fitting the cover to the book. With the right side of the fabric to the cover of the book, fold the 4-inch excess to the inside of the cover and pin along the top and bottom for a snug fit. Stitch, trim close to the seam, and turn right side out. Hand finish the hem along the remaining top and bottom edges. Sew a ribbon tie to the middle of each cover edge. Slip the book inside the slipcover and close the tie with a bow.

mother's day

The
CANDY CALENDAR

Being a collection of
150 pure candy recipes
for home cookery
arranged by months

Child's Silhouette

*Preserve the memory of childhood
with these hand-cut silhouettes.*

Seat your child in front of a bright light and take a snapshot of her profile. Trace the profile onto a piece of vellum tracing paper. Use a copy machine to enlarge this to the size you want and print extra copies. Put one copy onto a sheet of black fade-proof paper. With an X-acto® knife or fine scissors, cut out the silhouette carefully through both pieces of paper. If necessary, use the extra copies to repeat the process until you are satisfied with the likeness. Mount the black silhouette on white or light-colored mat board before framing.

Painted Bottles

*Create a dressing table set for Mother
with paints and pretty glass bottles.*

These inexpensive, sculptured bottles came from the import store. Choose a set of bottles with shapes that work well together. For best results, use permanent acrylic enamel paints and one basic design pattern that you can adapt to the shape of each bottle. The black dotted band along with the richly colored red and rose colors unifies the set shown here, but any design will work. Wash and dry the glass and then just paint on your design with a fine-tipped brush. Before the paint is dry, you can wipe away any mistakes. Enjoy the experiment!

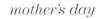

mother's day

HEAL THE PAST;
LIVE THE PRESENT;
DREAM THE FUTURE.

five.
GRADUATION

Ready to Go

Graduation is quite a milestone for parents and children.
Something handmade from home is an enduring reminder of the love that will always be there.

Cutouts and world maps bring new excitement to an old suitcase. Apply them with thinned wallpaper paste or another decoupage medium you prefer. Be sure all the map edges are carefully glued down before you add smaller cutouts to accent the maps. Seal the finished work with acrylic sealer and consider making a gift tag with a map drawn to show the way back home.

Treasure Box

In the dorm or first apartment,
the graduate will cherish this decorated box
as a place to keep personal treasures.

An older wooden box from the thrift shop is enhanced with cutouts from magazines and catalogs that reflect the collecting interests of the graduate. Decoupaged onto the wood with wallpaper paste, they are protected with several layers of acrylic sealer. If you wish, line the inside of the box with rectangles of green felt—cut to fit and glued to the sides and bottom. This adds a traditional look and feel to the finished box.

Weekend Duffel

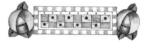

*Stitch up this easy duffel
and make weekend trips home a cinch.*

Inspired by a small remnant of vintage bark cloth, this bag used the piece to full advantage. Sew a 32-inch x 22-inch high rectangle of heavy fabric into a tube and make a circular bottom for the tube from the same or a matching fabric. Repeat this for a lining and insert the unturned lining into the bag. Sew a 3-inch wide strap that reaches from the bottom of the side seam beyond the top edge by 2 inches (about 24 inches total). Securely stitch one end of the strap to the bag bottom and then slip the unfinished strap end through a bangle bracelet. Stitch the strap end to the bag top and then blindstitch the lining to the bag around the top edge. When finished use the bracelet to close the bag by dropping it over the gathered edges of the top.

graduation

Let the Magic Begin!

six.
BRIDAL

Romantic Gift Box

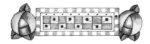

*An elaborate gift wrap becomes a keepsake
in itself with these artful touches.*

I magine the anticipation created with this lovely
gift box. Begin with a hatbox or another suitable
gift box and cover the top and bottom separately
with a decorative paper and lace trims as ribbons.
The bow is the central point of interest and decoration. Embellished with a silk gardenia and tumbling
strings of faux-pearls and flowers, this box charac-
terizes all the dreamy romance of the day.

Ring Bearer's Pillow

*An heirloom wedding handkerchief
reappears as a nostalgic pillow covering.
The crisp simplicity of this pillow
belies its powerful sentiment.*

Lay the handkerchief out flat and fold the corners
into the center so that they meet in the middle.
Measure the outside edges of this new square. Using a
pretty contrasting fabric, make a small pillow to these
measurements. Open the hankie and place the pillow in
the center on a 45 degree angle. Draw the corners of the
hankie up around the sides of the pillow and tack in the
center. Secure with generous lengths of ribbon tied as
for a package. The ribbon streamers can be looped
through the rings. A fresh blossom from the garden
adds a lovely fragrance and color.

Wedding Album

*Create a singular bridal scrapbook
with ribbons and rosebuds.*

A simple spiral journal is banded with stripes of
ribbon and lace trims carefully glued to the
front. A hand-lettered title framed with ribbon flowers, pearl beads, and silk leaves finishes the cover.
Disguise the spiral with a corded tassel and a few
more silk flowers, and this will become a treasured
record of the occasion.

Keepsake Box

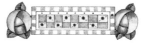

*Memorialize the day
with a decorated keepsake box.*

There are so many precious souvenirs of a wedding day that a place made especially for these keepsakes is a wonderful gift for the bride and groom. A wooden dresser box decorated with floral cutouts is a perfect setting for the wedding invitation, which can be decoupaged there as well. As always, seal your finished work with several layers of acrylic sealer. Glue a layer of felt to the bottom of the box so that it will not scratch fine furniture.

Bridesmaid's Gift

Thank your bridesmaid for her love and support with this sweetly trimmed hand mirror.

A pretty crocheted doily sets the stage on the back of a hand mirror. Glue it down and then add your favorite trimmings. Use a crafter's frame to quickframe a snapshot of the two of you. Apply silk flowers and leaves below the frame to dress it up. A few heart charms add more decoration and sentiment.

Bride and Groom Collection

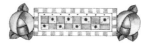

*Bridal collectibles punctuate a room
with nostalgia and charm.*

This is a fun collection to build, and it's a perfect complement to a collection of little curio shelves acquired over the years. Dressing room walls dotted with the various couples always seem to make room for one more pair. This would be a sweet way to celebrate anniversaries: adding each year to the collection and reliving the heartfelt vows and memories of the day.

Contributors

Project Designs

Mary Engelbreit: Porch Perches, Home Tweet Home, Holiday Collecting, Mother Dear, Romantic Gift Box

Charlotte Lyons: Sun Hat, Gardener's Basket, Cookie Pot, Easter Bonnet, Handkerchief Collar, Bunny Purse, Sweetheart Pin, Cookbook Slipcover, Painted Bottles, Spring Wreath, Treasure Box, Weekend Duffel, Tea Cozy, Ring Bearer's Pillow

Joseph Slattery: Easter Eggs, Wedding Album, Bridesmaid's Gift

Michael Mahler: Watering Can, Ready to Go Luggage

Cathy Pinter: Keepsake Box

Project Designs-continued

Alexa Anderson: Easter Cupcakes

Nicki Dwyer: Frosted Easter Cookies

Leslie Seith: May Basket

Sonja Willman: Mother's Day Breakfast

Jeff O'Connor: Child's Silhouette

Jesse Hickman: Porch Perches

Karen Foss: Bride and Groom Collection

Rhonda Cassidy: Holiday Collecting

Grateful Appreciation to

Rhonda and Doug Cassidy
Sonja and Robert Willman
Karen Foss and Jim Whitely
Jean Lowe, Stephanie Raaf, Stephanie Barken,
and Dave Bari

Index